Look After Yourself

Your Body

Look After Yourself

Your Body

Claire Llewellyn

SEA-TO-SEA

Mankato Collingwood London

This edition first published in 2008 by
Sea-to-Sea Publications
1980 Lookout Drive
North Mankato
Minnesota 56003

Library of Congress Cataloging in Publication Data

Llewellyn, Claire.
    Your body / by Claire Llewellyn.
        p.cm. -- (Look after yourself)
    ISBN 978-1-59771-096-1
    1. Body, Human--Juvenile literature. 2. Health--Juvenile
literature. 3. Hygiene--Juvenile literature. I. Title.

QP37.L625 2007
612--dc22

                                                      2006051279

9 8 7 6 5 4 3 2

Published by arrangement with the Watts Publishing Group Ltd, London.

Series editor: Sarah Peutrill
Design: Kirstie Billingham

Illustrations: James Evans
Photographs: Ray Moller unless otherwise acknowledged
Picture research: Diana Morris
Series consultant: Lynn Huggins-Cooper

Acknowledgments:
Biophoto Associates/SPL: 23tr
Layne Kennedy/Corbisstockmarket: 19
Brian Mitchell/Photofusion: 23bl

With thanks to our models: Aaron, Charlotte, Connor, Jake, Holly, and Nadine

Contents

Looking after yourself

Your body is working all the time. You need to look after it.

Treat your body well.

When we are very young, our parents look after us.

As we grow older, we can do more for ourselves.

We learn to take care of our bodies.

Keeping clean

You need to wash when you get up in the morning.

Remember to keep your hands and nails clean.

By the evening, your skin is dirty again.

Washing is fun!

Who wants to be smelly?

Take a shower or a bath.

Teeth, hair, and nails

Brushing your teeth helps keep them clean. It also helps stop tooth decay.

You need to wash your hair once or twice a week.

Short nails are easier to keep clean.

Germs can spread

Germs can spread from person to person and make you sick.

Washing your hands with soap can stop germs from spreading.

Use a hanky to stop cold germs from spreading.

Always catch your sneeze in a hanky.

Staying in shape

Exercise is very good for your body.

Skipping gets you in shape!

It makes your muscles bigger and your bones stronger. It helps keep you in shape!

I'm strong!

A good rest

Our bodies like to exercise, but they also need to rest.

Sleep rests every part of your body. It makes you good as new.

I love my bed!

Feeling unwell

Rest and sleep help you get better from illness.

I'm staying in bed.

Sometimes we need to see a doctor.

They can help us get better.

You will soon feel better.

Keeping safe

Sometimes we need medicines to make us well.

Beware! Some medicines look like candies.

Never take medicine unless a doctor or an adult gives it to you.

Glossary

diet The food and drink that you usually eat.

doctor A person whose job is to try and make sick people get better.

energy The power we get from food, which makes us able to work and grow, and keep warm.

exercise To be active.

germs Tiny living things that can spread disease and make you feel unwell. Germs are too small to see.

graze When you scrape your skin.

healthy Fit and well.

illness Being unwell.

medicine A liquid or tablet you take to make you well.

plaster cast A mold that holds a broken bone in place, so it can mend.

scab A hard crust that covers a cut or graze while it is healing.

sugar Something that is found in many foods and makes them taste sweet.

tooth decay When teeth get holes in them.

x-ray A special photograph that shows the bones inside you.

Index

About this book

Learning the principles of how to keep healthy and clean is one of life's most important skills. **Look After Yourself** is a series aimed at young children who are just beginning to develop these skills. **Your Body** looks at cleanliness and keeping the body healthy.

Here are a number of activities that children could try:

Pages 6-7 Discuss all the things they can do on their own. How much has changed since they were babies?

Pages 8-9 Test some different soaps and shower gels. Which creates a lather most quickly? Which has the nicest smell?

Pages 10-11 Make a poster to explain the ways we can avoid germs.

Pages 12-13 If appropriate, look at and test different nail scissors and cutters. Which is the easiest to use?

Pages 14-15 Write about the last time they were unwell. How did they feel? What and who helped them get better?

Pages 16-17 Write a menu for one day. Make sure it contains a variety of foods from all the food groups.

Pages 18-19 Devise and play some games with friends that use lots of energy. Afterward, decide which game was the most tiring. Why?

Pages 20-21 Find out how many hours of sleep different people in a family get. Who has the most sleep? Who has the least? Discuss why this is.

Pages 22-23 Discuss why cuts, grazes, and other accidents can be painful—the body is warning that something is wrong.

Pages 24-25 Make a list of all the qualities a doctor needs. Which is the most important?

Pages 26-27 Discuss where we get medicines from (i.e the pharmacy.)